# Poetry for Students, Volume 10

*Staff*

**Series Editor:** Michael L. LaBlanc.

**Contributing Editors:** Elizabeth Bellalouna, Anne Marie Hacht, Kimberly Hazelmyer, Mark Milne, Jennifer Smith.

**Managing Editor:** Dwayne Hayes.

**Research:** Victoria B. Cariappa, *Research Manager.* Cheryl Warnock, *Research Specialists.* Tamara Nott, Tracie A. Richardson, *Research Associates.* Nicodemus Ford, Sarah Genik, Timothy Lehnerer, *Research Assistants.*

**Permissions:** Maria Franklin, *Permissions Manager.* Sarah Tomasek, *Permissions Associate.*

**Manufacturing:** Mary Beth Trimper, *Manager, Composition and Electronic Prepress.* Evi Seoud, *Assistant Manager, Composition Purchasing and Electronic Prepress.* Stacy Melson, *Buyer.*

**Imaging and Multimedia Content Team:** Barbara Yarrow, *Manager.* Randy Bassett, *Imaging Supervisor.* Robert Duncan, Dan Newell, *Imaging Specialists.* Pamela A. Reed, *Imaging Coordinator.* Leitha Etheridge-Sims, Mary Grimes, *Image Catalogers.* Robyn Young, *Project Manager.* Dean Dauphinais, *Senior Image Editors.* Kelly A. Quin, *Image Editor.*

**Product Design Team:** Kenn Zorn, *Product Design Manager.* Pamela A. E. Galbreath, *Senior Art Director.* Michael Logusz, *Graphic Artist.*

## *Copyright Notice*

Since this page cannot legibly accommodate all copyright notices, the acknowledgments constitute an extension of the copyright notice.

While every effort has been made to secure permission to reprint material and to ensure the reliability of the information presented in this publication, Gale Research neither guarantees the accuracy of the data contained herein nor assumes any responsibility for errors, omissions, or discrepancies. Gale accepts no payment for listing; and inclusion in the publication of any organization, agency, institution, publication, service, or individual does not imply endorsement of the editors or publisher. Errors brought to the attention of the publisher and verified to the satisfaction of the publisher will be corrected in future editions.

This publication is a creative work fully protected by all applicable copyright laws, as well as by misappropriation, trade secret, unfair competition, and other applicable laws. The authors and editors of this work have added value to the underlying factual material herein through one or more of the following: unique and original selection, coordination, expression, arrangement, and classification of the information. All rights to this publication will be vigorously defended.

Copyright © 2001
Gale Group
27500 Drake Rd.
Farmington Hills, MI 48331-3535

All rights reserved including the right of reproduction in whole or in part in any form.

ISBN 0-7876-3571-5
ISSN 1094-7019

Printed in Canada
10 9 8 7 6 5 4 3 2 1

# *Dulce et Decorum Est*

**Wilfred Owen**

*1920*

## Introduction

Many of Wilfred Owen's poems, including "Dulce et Decorum Est," paint in stark images the brutality of war. Having fought in some of the bloodiest action of World War I, Owen wished to warn his English countrymen that the horrors of combat far outweigh its glory. He believed that those writers and politicians at home who championed the necessity of war did so only because they had not experienced its suffering—the suffering of the poem's dying soldier poisoned by mustard gas, his "white eyes writhing in his face," the blood "gargling" from his lungs. Such images were intended to make civilians experience the troops' fear and pain. Owen hoped that by displaying in such vivid terms the reality of war he might encourage others to let pity inform their patriotism.

"Dulce et Decorum Est," like much of Owen's work, relies on irony—a figure of speech in which the actual intent is expressed in words which carry the opposite meaning—to help convey its message about war. An example of this is title itself, from the Latin poet Horace: *"Dulce et decorum est pro patria mori"* ("Sweet and fitting it is to die for one's country"). Although patriotic and romantic depiction's of war run through British poetry of the Victorian period (see, for instance, Tennyson's "The Charge of the Light Brigade"), Owen hoped to direct poetry in a new direction. He shows us nothing "sweet" in a gas attack, nothing "fitting" or heroic about bootless, "blood-shod" soldiers marching "like old beggars" and "coughing like hags." Compared with war's absurd violence, Owen suggests, patriotism becomes an absurd matter: the poem never tells us what country the poisoned soldier is dying for.

Owen himself was killed in 1918, a week before the armistice that ended World War I. He had just returned to the front after recuperating from illness in a Scottish hospital. While in the hospital, he met and was encouraged by the English poet Siegfried Sassoon, who published much of Owen's work in a volume titled *Poems* in 1920. Today Owen is regarded as one of the finest war poets of the century.

## Author Biography

Owen was born in 1893 in Oswestry, Shropshire, the eldest son of Susan Shaw Owen and Thomas Owen, a railroad station master. After attending schools in Birkenhead and Shrewsbury, and failing in an attempt to win a scholarship to enter London University, Owen became an unpaid lay assistant to the Vicar of Dunsden in Oxfordshire. After trying unsuccessfully for a scholarship again in 1913, he spent time in France, teaching for a year at the Berlitz School of Languages in Bordeaux, and then privately tutoring for an additional year. Shortly after his return to England, Owen enlisted in the Artist's Rifles. He was later commissioned as a lieutenant in the Manchester Regiment, and in late 1916, with World War I raging, was posted to the Western Front, where he participated in the Battle of the Somme. Suffering shell-shock after several months of service at the front, Owen was declared unfit to command and was taken out of action in May, 1917. In June he was admitted to Craiglockhart War Hospital in Edinburgh, where he met Siegfried Sassoon, an outspoken critic of the war who encouraged him to use his battle experiences as subjects for poetry. Owen returned to the front in early September 1918, shortly afterwards being awarded the Military Cross for gallantry. He was killed in action at the Sambre Canal in northeast France on November 4, 1918—one week before the Armistice. He is buried at Ors, France.

Sassoon's respect and encouragement confirmed for Owen his ability as a poet. Under Sassoon's guidance he first adapted his poetic techniques to nontraditional war subjects, writing most of his critically acclaimed poems in the fifteen months prior to his death. Having had only five poems published during his lifetime, Owen's reputation as a poet was only established in 1920, with the publication of *Poems*, a volume edited by Sassoon. A second collection edited by Edmund Blunden caught the attention of W. H. Auden and the poets in his circle who admired Owen's artistry and technique. Owen is widely considered among the finest English poets of World War I, gaining further recognition through an additional collection edited by C. Day Lewis and the inclusion of his works in numerous anthologies.

# Poem Summary

## Lines 1-4

In contrast with the title, which suggests that war, patriotic duty, and even death for one's country are "sweet and fitting," the poet shows us nothing noble about the wretched condition of the soldiers on their march. These troops appear far different than the ones the British people might have been used to reading about. They are "bent double" under the weight of their packs, but bent also, perhaps, under the weight of duty itself. Using simile—a figure of speech expressing the similarity between two seemingly unlike things—the speaker compares the troops to "old beggars" and "hags." The effect of the comparisons is to create a frightful, almost medieval atmosphere. Moreover, the comparison of the soldiers with "hags," or witches, creates the sense of the unnatural and introduces the possibility of some kind of evil at hand. The "haunting fires" reinforce this sense. Also notice, beginning the second line, the sequence of participles—"knock-kneed, coughing," etc.—that suggest the sounds and persistence of battle.

## Line 2

In the second line, the speaker defines his relationship to the situation: "we cursed through sludge." By identifying himself as one of the soldiers, he establishes the authority necessary to comment on the hardships he describes. In addition, he reminds us that war is not a far-away spectacle, not the heroic scene described by Tennyson in "The Charge of the Light Brigade," but as real and as close to us as the speaker himself.

## *Lines 5-8*

The speaker lists the soldiers' tribulations in short, direct phrases, varying at times from the dominant iambic meter to highlight certain details. A number of figurative uses are introduced here as well to demonstrate the suffering of the troops. They are "blood-shod"—a use of metaphor since it is an implied, rather than directly stated, comparison between the blood on the troops' feet and the boots they have "lost." Also note a similar use of hyperbole—a figure of speech based on exaggeration—when the speaker says the men are "deaf" to the cries of their comrades and that "all went lame; all blind." The troops are "drunk with fatigue"— an ironic echo of the "sweetness" in the title. Even the falling artillery shells, or "Five-Nines," are "tired" and "outstripped" by the grave nature of the men's fatigue. The images presented thus far create a somber, static, and miserable world, one in which the indignities the soldiers suffer seem as if they will go on indefinitely. This stasis, however, provides a grim contrast with the explosive violence of the second stanza.

## *Lines 9-11*

A shift in voice brings on the sudden gas attack. In two sharp syllables someone—we cannot tell who—warns the men of a gas attack. We watch the men scramble for their gas masks in "an ecstasy of fumbling." Owen might intend irony in the use of the word "ecstasy," which can mean "a frenzy of exalted delight." Certainly the men should not be delighted about the attack. In an older sense of the word, however, Owen might simply mean that the soldiers have entered a state of emotion so intense that rational thought is obliterated. A third possibility is that Owen is suggesting a kind of mystical experience. As the men fight for their lives, they may feel the kind of religious ecstasy associated with near-death experiences. At any rate, one soldier fails to put his mask on in time and is poisoned by the gas.

## *Lines 12-14*

In World War I both the allies and the Germans used mustard gas as a way of both attacking and striking fear into the enemy. If breathed without the protection of a mask, the gas quickly burns away the lining of the respiratory system. Thus the speaker compares the soldier with a man consumed in "fire or lime." Such a fate is not often compared with "drowning," yet the speaker knows that victims of mustard gas effectively drown in the blood from their own lung tissues. In addition, mustard gas has a particular hue—"as under a green sea." The speaker views the "flound'ring" man as if through an underwater mask, adding to the nightmarish and surreal atmosphere of the poem thus far.

## *Lines 15-16*

In these two lines the incident is transformed to one that seems like a dream to an actual dream— a recurring vision or nightmare that the speaker cannot escape. In this dream the "guttering, choking" soldier "plunges" at the "helpless" speaker, seeking assistance. Although the speaker can do nothing for the man, there is still a feeling of responsibility and guilt. Perhaps many survivors of such attacks felt the same sense of guilt, wondering why they lived while their friends died.

## *Lines 17-24*

In this last stanza the speaker directly addresses the reader—one who, presumably, is reading in the safety of England and who has not personally witnessed the type of horror just described. The speaker suggests that if the reader too were subject to such memories, they would "smother" the reader's conscience in the same way the mustard gas has suffocated the soldier. The images that follow depict the aftermath of the attack: the soldier's slow death, the "eyes writhing" in his face, the "blood come gargling from his lungs." Note among these descriptions the powerful use of alliteration, or the repetition of initial consonant sounds in closely related words. A good example of this can be found in lines 18 and 19: "wagon," watch," white," "writhing." The speaker combines this sound device with the most discomforting words he can conjure. The soldier's face is like "a devil's sick of sin"; his lungs are "corrupted" and "obscene as cancer, bitter as the cud / of vile incurable sores on innocent tongues" that suggest unseemly diseases.

## *Lines 25-28*

If the reader—"my friend"—could see such horrors, the speaker insists, then his or her attitude toward war would change. The reader would not encourage war-like fervor, would not repeat patriotic slogans such as *Dulce et decorum est / pro patria mori*, a saying which would have been familiar to Owen's contemporaries. In this part of the poem, the Latin phrase is used without irony: it is simply called a "Lie." Owen suggests that if the reader continue to spread that lie to young men prone to believing romantic sentiment, then those young men will likely receive a fate like that of the fallen soldier. Thus the final line is the shortest of the poem, bringing on the full effect of the three crucial words, *Pro patria mori:* to die for one's country.

## Media Adaptations

- The audiobook *English Verse: Early 20th Century from Hardy to Owen* covers the great English poetry written from 1880-1918, including the "poignant realism of the War Poets Rupert Brooke, Wilfred Owen, and Siegfried Sassoon." The audio anthology is published by Penguin Audiobooks.

- Created in 1999, the on-line Wilfred Owen Association at http://www.wilfred.owen.association.mc offers visitors a virtual tour of Owen's life and poetry. There is also a membership offer, including a twice-a-year newsletter.

- Another website— http://www.hcu.ox.uk/jtap/— with

information on Wilfred Owen is the Wilfred Owen Multimedia Digital Archive (WOMDA). Created by the Humanities Computing Unit at Oxford University, this site includes not only Owen's manuscripts, but also has a selection of World War I publications and an archive of period documents.

- Artist Robert Andrew Parker has created an exhibition based on the poems of Wilfred Owen. Published in catalog format by the Saint Paul Art Center in Saint Paul, Minnesota, the title of the portfolio is *Watercolors by Robert Andrew Parker: My Subject is War and the Pity of War*.

## Themes

### *Death and Human Suffering*

Owen's poem, describing the death of a soldier caught in a gas attack, is at once a realistic portrait of the brutality of war and a lesson in morality to those who would romanticize patriotic duty.

## Topics for Further Study

- Contrast a poem of Owen's to Richard Lovelace's "To Lucasta," a poem that expresses the honor of being called to military duty. How does tone (the speaker's attitude) help create the vastly different themes in each poem?

- Trace the developments of modern warfare from World War I to today. What major technologies have helped define warfare along the way?
- Research the effects mustard gas has on the human body. Include various systems (e.g. nervous, respiratory, etc.).
- Think of an abstract concept (like Love, Hate, Death, Confusion, etc.). Now, without naming the abstract concept, write a poem describing it, using only concrete sensory details (sight, sound, smell, taste, and touch). When finished, share your poem with a classmate and see if they can tell you what you've written your poem about.
- As a class, create your own War Memorial. Include family members and friends of families who have served during wartime. You may also add artists like Wilfred Owen, Yusef Komunyakaa, Tim O'Brien, John Singer Sargent, and others. Be creative! Include photos, poems, letters, artwork, *etc.*

---

Owen's representation of death and human suffering within the poem is significant in terms of its depth; on the surface the poem chronicles the physical destruction of men at war. "Dulce et Decorum Est" achieves its power, however, through the equally compelling discussion of both the emotional and spiritual destruction with which war threatens the individual.

Death and human suffering, on a purely physical plane, are abundant throughout the poem. The first stanza depicts the horrors of the war on the human body-even for those lucky enough to survive their tour of duty. It takes young, healthy, empowered men and turns them, metaphorically, into aged transients and pathetic invalids. War has exacted such a physical price on those asked to wage it that they are literally transformed with exhaustion, unable to appreciate the deadly reality surrounding them. They are, in Owen's words, "… Drunk with fatigue; deaf even to the hoots / Of gas-shells dropping softly behind." The remaining lines of the poem focus on the horrific death of one young man caught in the devastating fumes of mustard gas. Owen's use of water imagery makes this scene all the more uncomfortable to witness, as the soldier's death is compared to a drowning. He is described as "flound'ring," "guttering," and "choking." Owen twice uses the very word —"drowning."

While the physical pain is noteworthy, the death of the soldier is rivaled by the emotional suffering present in the poem. The men themselves face the most primal of emotions, fear. First, Owen repeats the word "gas" at the beginning of the second stanza; the capitalization of all three letters in its second usage clearly indicates a heightened sense of panic. Interestingly, while the impact of the poem in no small measure comes from the candid nature of its witness, the narrator does not need to embellish the account with exaggerated punctuation. The images speak for themselves. It is only here, as the reader hears the dialogue of the soldiers, that we see the use of exclamation points. This combined with the aforementioned use of capitalization serves to convey a strong emotional investment. The true emotional impact, though, is on the solitary soldier. It is not, however, to be focused on the dying man, whose terrified confusion can easily be imagined in "the white eyes writhing in his face." It is on the man condemned to replay this grisly scene again and again in his tortured sleep. The speaker in "Dulce et Decorum Est," so clearly identifiable as Owen himself, is forever plagued with visions of his comrade's demise, evidenced by lines 15-16: "In all my dreams before my helpless sight/He plunges at me, guttering, choking, drowning" Just as there was nothing either man could do to prevent the gas from killing the soldier once he has inhaled the noxious fumes, the guilt-stricken speaker seems equally incapable of forgetting what he has seen in surviving the attack. The soldier's literal death—suffocation by "froth-corrupted lungs"—is symbolically preserved in the speaker's "smothering dreams."

Finally, the poem revolves around spiritual suffering and death. Owen once described himself as "a conscientious objector with a very seared conscience," further stating that "pure Christianity will not fit with pure patriotism." There is a distinct irony that should be acknowledged here. Owen's reputation as a poet is a direct result of the impact the war had on his poetry. While his earlier work evidences a commitment to the Romantic precepts of Love and Beauty and the trappings of fantasy, it is his role as a soldier in one of the most costly wars in the history of mankind that reveals his true growth as an artist. War confronted Owen with reality, with Truth; however, these same horrible realities that signal a maturation for the poet, also coincide with the destructive force the war had on all who fought it. For Owen, the war became a symbol for the ugliness of human nature. The last stanza, then, represents for the speaker a sacrifice, with the doomed soldier's face "hanging … like a devil's sick of sin." The death is "Obscene," compared to "vile, incurable sores on innocent tongues." These comparisons are not those of the man who is dying, but instead of the man left to remember the death. In the end, it is the poet's innocence—his tongue—which has been violated. It is his responsibility to at once reveal the ugly truth of war to the world, and warn others of the danger of romanticizing this truth. In one stanza Owen connects the guilt a surviving soldier feels when his brother-in-arms falls with the guilt others should feel who either ignore or willfully dismiss the truth of war.

## Style

"Dulce et Decorum Est" is divided into four stanzas, each addressing situation or idea. The first stanza describes a group of marching soldiers in a shell-shocked, wretched condition. The second stanza shows a gas attack in which one of the soldiers is stricken. The third stanza describes the event's nightmarish effect on the speaker, while the fourth suggests that the reader should be similarly impacted.

The dominant meter of the poem is iambic. This means the poem's lines are constructed in two-syllable segments, called iambs, in which the first syllable is unstressed and the second stressed. As an example of iambic meter, consider the following line from the poem:

> Till on the haunting flares we turned
> our backs.

If we divide the iambs from one another and mark the unstressed and stressed syllables, the line appears like this:

> Tillon *the haun* ting flares *we turned*
> our backs.

Reading the line normally, you will notice the emphasis on the stressed syllables. Iambic meter is natural to the English language and is the most common measure in English verse. Shakespeare employed iambic meter throughout much of his work. In fact, to remember what iambic meter is, you can always sound out the syllables of these famous words: "To be, or not to be."

While "Dulce et Decorum Est" is written primarily in iambic meter, Owen deviates from the pattern at times to heighten the sense of certain words. Consider, for example, this line:

> But limped on, blood-shod. All went lame; all
> blind;

If you read the line naturally, you will find only one weak, or unstressed, syllable: the first. All others are strong, or stressed, in order point out the crippling reality of the soldiers' physical condition. The poet varies his iambic meter in lines like this to achieve a specific effect. Yet to do so, he has had to set up a dominant pattern from which to deviate.

Finally, note that the poem's stanzas include quatrains, or groups of four lines each, in which the last syllables of first and third lines as well as the second and fourth lines rhyme with one another. This form of rhyme scheme is often used in ballads and in heroic verse. Owen might have chosen the form to make readers think about the contrast between his poem and more traditional war poems.

## Historical Context

"Dulce et Decorum Est" is historically useful because it so poignantly shows both the changes in the way war was to be fought as well as the necessary metamorphosis war poetry would have to undergo in the face of such change. To understand this, it is vital to consider the two major differences the twentieth century brought on to the battle field —namely, technology and trenches.

It has been estimated by war historian Leon Woolf that somewhere in the neighborhood of 10,000,000 men died fighting in World War I. This does not include the 21,000,000 soldiers wounded, and only accounts for a million of the 7,750,919 captured or missing in action. While such numbers are certainly staggering, none include the loss of civilian life during the war. It is under this dark umbrella that Wilfred Owen both fought, wrote, and died. The numbers alone would seem to support Owen's caustic message in "Dulce et Decorum Est"; anyone witnessing such a tremendous loss of life would be hard put to continue feeding young children the romantic rhetoric of patriotism and heroism associated with warfare going into the twentieth century. But what caused such loss? Simply put, mankind became more efficient. The Great War was the first war in which technology was implemented in order to achieve military objectives. Men were equipped with machine guns, capable of spraying the enemy with bullets; the battlefields were bombarded with explosives and gas shells. And with this efficiency, this speed of death, came the demise of the romantic notion of the war hero. As Arthur E. Lane writes in his book *An Adequate Response:* The war was a lesson in humility, not an exercise in cultural style: death came unseen and from a distance, and the inoffensive ex-clerk in an ill-fitting uniform who dutifully placed shell after shell in the breechlock of a gun which pointed only at the sky never knew if heroes or cowards or corpses awaited dismemberment in the distance. Men died asleep or playing cards, eating breakfast, writing letters, quarreling, picking lice from their clothes and hair. They died praying or cursing, weeping or dumb with horror, comforting each other or fighting for shelter.

## Compare & Contrast

- **November 11, 1918:** The Armistice agreement is signed at 5:50 a.m.; at 11:00 a.m. all fighting ceases. World War I is over.

  **September 1939:** The German attack on Poland precipitates World War II. Over 6,000,000 Jews and millions of others will be persecuted and murdered under Nazi tyranny.

  **May 8, 1945:** Germany surrenders to Allied forces.

**August 6, 1945:** The first atomic bomb to be dropped on Japan is dropped on Hiroshima.

**August 9, 1945:** The second atomic bomb to be dropped on Japan is dropped on Nagasaki. The Japanese surrender September 2, 1945, bringing an end to World War II.

**June 1950:** The North Korean army launches a surprise attack on the thirty-eighth parallel, marking the beginning of the Korean War.

**July 27, 1953:** The Armistice signed in Panmunjon brings an end to the Korean War.

**March 8, 1965:** The first American combat troops land in Da Nang, Vietnam, marking the "Americanization" of the war in Vietnam.

**1968:** The number of American forces in Vietnam reaches over 500,000. Over 14,000 U.S. soldiers will be killed in 1968.

**March 28, 1973:** The Last of the American troops and prisoners leave South Vietnam. The United States has lost over 45,000 men killed in action and a further 300,000 have been wounded.

**1982:** The Vietnam Veteran's Memorial—"The Wall"—is dedicated in Washington, D.C.

**1990-2000:** Wars continue to be waged, throughout the world and for a myriad of different reasons. From the Persian Gulf War to the warfare in Bosnia-Herzegovina, peoples of the world continue to fight each other.

---

Owen captures this in his poem, too. There are no heroes, only dog-tired men struggling for survival. None knew where the "tired, outstripped Five-Nines" were fired from, and most only have time to retreat beneath the relative safety of their gas masks before it is too late. Owen does not depict the men valiantly overcoming the effects of the gas to help their dying comrade. This is dirt-level survival. This is life on the battlefield. The cost is great and Owen reflects the sheer volume of death wrought by the war when he describes the way the men treated the dying soldier. There is no time for tears; last rites are muffled beneath panes of glass and clouds of gas. The soldiers merely fling him in a wagon. In the end, no one can claim heroism—not the unknown man shelling them, not the unfortunate soldier left to die, and certainly not the guilt-ridden witness whose only response is to follow behind the wagon as the rest of the troops retreat from danger.

Just as the *way* in which war was fought forced a change in poetic perception, so too did *where* it was fought. The use of trenches is yet another hallmark of World War I. Wet, cold, and muddy, there was no retreat for the men forced to endure these conditions. In *The Truth of War*, author Desmond Graham writes of this harsh reality: "Physically, despite the inaction, the soldier is still assaulted, by cold; and physically, just as mentally, he is not left alone but reminded of his defencelessness by the snow which reaches his face. In this state, dreams do remain, and the soldier succumbs to them." While Graham is specifically relating to Owen's poem "Exposure"—a detailed account of life in the trenches—the same realities are reflected in "Dulce et Decorum Est" The reader can clearly see the effects living and fighting in the trenches has had on the men in the first stanza. They are not under direct military attack, and yet are "bent double" and "coughing like hags." Owen makes mention of "the sludge" in which they march, some without boots. Here, too, we see the devastating toll the exposure to the harsh climate has taken on the men before the gas attack even commences. Again, this is not a poem of heroism; it is a poem of fact.

# Critical Overview

Many writers, including the prominent British poet C. Day Lewis, have commented that Owen's war poems are among the best written in our century. Though Owen lived to see only four of his poems published, he wrote nearly all of his best work, including "Dulce et Decorum Est," in a span of only one year, the twenty-sixth and last year of his life. Lewis notes the maturity of these poems: "It was as if, during the weeks of his first tour of duty in the trenches, he came of age emotionally and spiritually." Lewis cites "the originality and force of [the poems'] language" as well as their passion and "harsh realism." "Dulce et Decorum Est" marks the period which, according to Lewis, made Owen a major poet capable of changing people's minds about war. The sudden maturation of Owen's work, writes Lewis, represents "a forced growth, a revolution in his mind which, blasting through all the poetic *brick-a-brack*, enabled him to see his subject clear—'War, and the pity of War.'"

Not all have agreed that "the pity of war"—Owen's own phrase—is a basis for sound poetry. William Butler Yeats, for one, determined the "passive suffering" in Owen's work an unfit theme. Critic Samuel Hazo has challenged the notion that many of the poems spring from pity at all. Instead, Hazo suggests, the bulk of Owen's work arises from uncontrolled indignation. "Many of them," he writes in *Renascence*, "are revelations of acrimony, protest, pessimism, outrage and hatred." While Hazo admits Owen manages to achieve a degree of objectivity in some poems, he finds "Dulce et Decorum Est" to be merely didactic. "Whatever is poetic in it," Hazo writes, "is subordinated to a rhetorical end."

## What Do I Read Next?

- Randall Jarrell is a writer who, like Owen, uses powerful imagery to convey the horror of war. His poem "Death of the Ball Turret Gunner," in particular, has themes and incidents similar to those in "Dulce et Decorum Est." Specifically, the reader is shown the fear and nightmarish reality surrounding a gunner's last living moments. The poem is included in Jarrell's 1945 collection, *The Complete Poems*.

- In the September 18, 1997 issue of *English in Australia* authors Peter McFarlane and Trevor Temple discuss an innovative plan for teaching Owen's poetry by having students develop meaning with a dramatic reading of the poem, interpretive music or dance, or artwork. McFarlane and Temple note that the method seems to have fostered for their students a better understanding and student "ownership" of Owen's poetry. The title of their article is "Making Meaning: A Teaching Approach to the Poetry of Wilfred Owen Using the Visual and Performing Arts."

- Vietnam veteran and poet Yusef Komunyakaa offers another excellent example of a soldier who recaptures "in country" experiences in his poetry. Like Owen, Komunyakaa saw fellow soldiers fall in action. His poem "Facing It" depicts the physical and emotional reflection a veteran has when visiting the Vietnam Veterans Memorial. This poem can be found in Komunyakaa's 1988 *Dien Kai Dau.*

- A true sense of the talent of an artist can not possibly be gained through the analysis of a single piece of that artist's craft. Students interested in Owen's poetry should read his other works, including "Anthem for Doomed Youth," "Strange Meeting," "Arms and the Boy," "Spring Offensive," and "A Terre." These poems and many others can be found in Owen's *Collected Poems*, published in 1964.

- R. L. Barth's 1983 *Forced Marching to the Styx: Vietnam War Poems* is yet another example of the impact war has on humanity. An excellent place to begin is with Barth's poem "The Insert."

- Students interested in the fiction arising from wartime experience should read the works of Tim O'Brien. An excellent place to start is O'Brien's 1979 National Book Award-winning novel *Going after Cacciato*.

# Sources

Blunden, Edmund, ed., *The Poems of Wilfred Owen*, New Directions Books, 1949.

Caesar, Adrian, "Wilfred Owen," in his *Taking It Like a Man: Suffering, Sexuality, and the War Poets*, Manchester University Press, 1993, pp. 115-171.

*'Dulce et Decorum Est'—A Literary Writer's Point of View*,www.writerswrite.com/journal/sept97/mika.htr (September 1997) Ellis, John, *Eye-Deep in Hell: Trench Warfare in World War I*, Pantheon Books, 1976.

Graham, Desmond, *The Truth of War*, Carcanet Press, 1984.

Hazo, Samuel J., "The Passion of Wilfred Owen," in *Renascence*, Vol. XI, Summer, 1959.

Hibberd, Dominic, *Owen the Poet*, The University of Georgia Press, 1986.

Kennedy, X. J., and Dana Gioia, eds., *Literature: An Introduction to Fiction, Poetry, and Drama*, Harper Collins, 1995.

Lane, Arthur E., *An Adequate Response: The War Poetry of Wilfred Owen & Siefried Sassoon*, Wayne State University Press, 1972.

Lewis, C. Day, introduction, in *The Collected Poems of Wilfred Owen*, edited by C. Day Lewis,

Chatto & Windus, 1963.

Lewis, C. Day, ed., *The Collected Poems of Wilfred Owen*, New Directions Books, 1964.

McPhail, Helen, and Philip Guest, *On the Trail of the Poets of the Great War*, LEO Cooper, 1998.

Newbolt, Henry, *The Later Life and Letters of Sir Henry Newbolt*, edited by Margaret Newbolt, Faber and Faber, 1942, p. 314.

Pope, Jessie, "A Cossack Charge," in her *Jessie Pope's War Poems*, Grant Richards, Ltd., 1915, p. 24.

Silkin, Jon, *Out of Battle: The Poetry of the Great War*, St. Martin's Press, Inc., 1998.

Tennyson, Alfred, "The Charge of the Light Brigade," in *The Norton Anthology of English Literature*, Edited by M. H. Abrams, Norton, 1993, pp. 1132-1133.

Welland, D. S. R., *Wilfred Owen: A Critical Study*, Chatto and Windus, 1960.

White, Gertrude M., ed., *Wilfred Owen*, Twayne Publishers, Inc., 1969.

Williams, Merryn, "Poetry," in her *Wilfred Owen*, Seren Books, 1993, pp. 46-114.

*The Works of Wilfred Owen with an Introduction and Bibliography*, The Wordsworth Poetry Library, 1994.

# For Further Study

McPhail, Helen, and Philip Guest, *On the Trail of the Poets of the Great War*, LEO Cooper, 1998.

> This book is a part of the Battleground Europe series, and provides not only a look at Owen's development as a poet, but offers a detailed timeline of his military career. Complete with photographs and correspondences, the text serves the historian or traveler as a guide to the battles and events that would be reflected so powerfully in Owen's poetry.

Welland, D. S. R., *Wilfred Owen: A Critical Study*, Chatto & Windus, 1960.

> This book remains a definitive look at the critical importance of Wilfred Owen's poetry. Welland offers insight into Owen's earlier, pre-war poetry; analyzes the effect his service in World War I had on his craft; and discusses Owen's place and reputation in the 20th century.

White, Gertrude M., ed., *Wilfred Owen*, Twayne Publishers, Inc., 1969.

> Much like Welland, White traces Owen's growth as a poet, discussing

his early work and the forces that brought about his poetic maturity. After a detailed study of Owen's work-including commentary on his early adherence to the Romantic tradition and the qualities, themes, techniques of his mature poetry- White too chronicles the growth of Owen's reputation following his death.

www.ingramcontent.com/pod-product-compliance
Ingram Content Group UK Ltd.
Pitfield, Milton Keynes, MK11 3LW, UK
UKHW051415110425
5444UKWH00027B/261